INCREDIBLE ANIMAL LIFE CYCLES
LIFE CYCLE OF A
LADYBUG

by Karen Latchana Kenney

pogo

Ideas for Parents and Teachers

Pogo Books let children practice reading informational text while introducing them to nonfiction features such as headings, labels, sidebars, maps, and diagrams, as well as a table of contents, glossary, and index.

Carefully leveled text with a strong photo match offers early fluent readers the support they need to succeed.

Before Reading

- "Walk" through the book and point out the various nonfiction features. Ask the student what purpose each feature serves.
- Look at the glossary together. Read and discuss the words.

Read the Book

- Have the child read the book independently.
- Invite him or her to list questions that arise from reading.

After Reading

- Discuss the child's questions. Talk about how he or she might find answers to those questions.
- Prompt the child to think more. Ask: What did you know about the life cycle of a ladybug before you read this book? What more would you like to learn after reading it?

Pogo Books are published by Jump!
5357 Penn Avenue South
Minneapolis, MN 55419
www.jumplibrary.com

Library of Congress Cataloging-in-Publication Data

Names: Kenney, Karen Latchana, author.
Title: Life cycle of a ladybug / by Karen Latchana Kenney.
Description: Minneapolis, MN : Jump!, Inc., [2018]
Series: Incredible animal life cycles
"Pogo Books are published by Jump!"
Audience: Ages 7-10. | Includes index.
Identifiers: LCCN 2017061422 (print)
LCCN 2017058430 (ebook)
ISBN 9781624968204 (ebook)
ISBN 9781624968181 (hardcover : alk. paper)
ISBN 9781624968198 (pbk.)
Subjects: LCSH: Ladybugs–Life cycles–Juvenile literature.
Beetles–Life cycles–Juvenile literature.
Classification: LCC QL596.C65 (print)
LCC QL596.C65 K4625 2018 (ebook) | DDC 595.76/9–dc23
LC record available at https://lccn.loc.gov/2017061422

Editor: Jenna Trnka
Book Designer: Molly Ballanger

Photo Credits: Serg64/Shutterstock, cover (left); Marek R. Swadzba/Shutterstock, cover (top right); Lee Hua Ming/Shutterstock, cover (bottom right); Protasov AN/Shutterstock, 1; Henrik Larsson/Shutterstock, 3; Nigel Cattlin/Alamy, 4; Mitsuhiko Imamori/Minden Pictures, 5, 16, 20-21; Bert Pijs/Minden Pictures/SuperStock, 6-7; Biosphoto/SuperStock, 8-9; XEG/Shutterstock, 10; defun/iStock, 11; Kim Taylor/Minden Pictures, 12-13; Tomatito/Shutterstock, 14-15; Zhukerman/Shutterstock, 17; Lamzinvnikola/Shutterstock, 18-19; Africa Studio/Shutterstock, 23.

Printed in the United States of America at Corporate Graphics in North Mankato, Minnesota.

TABLE OF CONTENTS

CHAPTER 1

LADYBUG LARVAE

Shiny, yellow ovals sit in rows. What are they? Ladybug eggs. They are safe under a leaf. But they are starting to change.

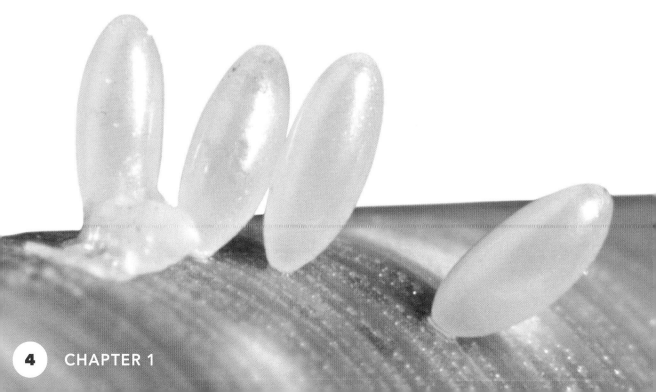

The eggs get darker. Then something moves inside each one. Watch! These ladybug eggs are about to **hatch**. The eggs split. Out pop the **larvae**. This is just one step in each ladybug's amazing life cycle.

larva

The larvae don't look like ladybugs at all. They have long, spiky bodies and six legs. Yet all ladybug larvae have one important task. They are hungry, and they need to eat.

DID YOU KNOW?

Not all ladybug larvae are black. The Australian ladybird is fuzzy and white. Ladybird is another name for ladybug.

Ladybug larvae eat aphids, spider mites, and scale bugs. The larvae eat and eat. They need the energy to grow.

DID YOU KNOW?

Farmers and gardeners love ladybugs. Why? Because ladybugs help them out. They eat bugs that kill plants.

aphid

CHAPTER 2

MOLTING INTO A PUPA

A larva keeps growing for the next few weeks. But its skin doesn't stretch. To get bigger, it needs to **molt**. It attaches its **abdomen** to a leaf. Then its skin begins to split.

It wriggles out from inside. The larva is bigger and light in color. Its color eventually darkens. Its skin hardens.

pupa

After three molts, the larva is ready for a bigger change. It attaches its abdomen to a leaf or a stem. Then it splits its skin one last time. Now it is a **pupa**.

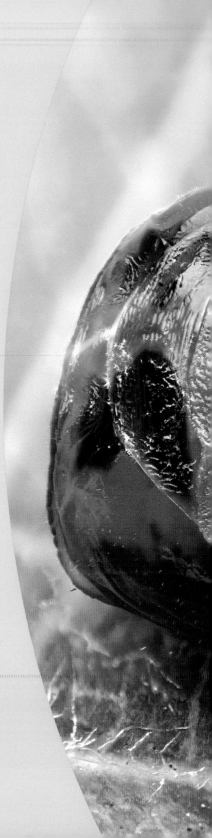

The pupa hunches over into a little mound. It will stay like this for about a week. The pupa does not eat or move much. Under its skin, the adult ladybug forms.

DID YOU KNOW?

The pupa can move if it senses danger. It shakes its body to scare off **predators**.

CHAPTER 3

READY TO FLY

The adult ladybug is about to break free. It has changed a lot inside the pupa. It pushes its way out and rests right by its old body. It is missing its spots, but they'll appear soon.

elytra

First the new adult needs to let its body dry. Its **elytra** make a hard case for its body. They protect papery wings underneath. Soon the ladybug will take flight.

In late summer, the adults eat for a few weeks. But they need to find a place to **hibernate**. They gather together in large groups. There might be hundreds or thousands of them. They keep each other warm. This is how they survive the cold winter.

TAKE A LOOK!

Each ladybug goes through a life cycle. It has four **stages**:

egg:
Around four days after it is laid, the egg hatches.

larva:
The larva grows and molts three times. This stage takes about 2 to 3 weeks.

pupa:
A fourth molt turns the larva into a pupa.

adult:
After about a week, the adult hatches. Adults live 1 to 3 years.

eggs

In the spring, ladybugs **mate**. A female lays her eggs on a leaf in an area where there is plenty of food. The ladybug life cycle continues.

ACTIVITIES & TOOLS

TRY THIS!

ORIGAMI WINGS

Ladybug wings fold up so small that scientists study them to see how they do it. See how small you can fold up wings with this activity.

What You Need:
- small pieces of square paper
- pencil
- scissors

1. Draw a wing shape on a few pieces of paper.

2. Cut out each wing.

3. Now try to fold one wing shape. Keep making folds until you have a small shape. Don't crumple up the paper!

4. Now try folding two more wing shapes. How small can you make them?

5. Compare your three folded wings. Which is the smallest? Unfold it to study your folds. Try again to see if you can fold a wing even smaller.

GLOSSARY

abdomen: The rear section of an insect's body.

elytra: The two wing cases of a ladybug or other kind of beetle.

hatch: To break out of an egg.

hibernate: To spend the winter in a deep sleep to save energy and survive cold temperatures.

larvae: Insects in a stage between egg and pupa.

mate: When a male and female animal or insect come together to make babies.

molt: To shed old skin or coverings to grow bigger.

predators: Animals that hunt other animals for food.

pupa: An insect in a stage between a larva and adult.

stages: Steps or periods of development.

INDEX

TO LEARN MORE

Learning more is as easy as 1, 2, 3.

1) Go to www.factsurfer.com

2) Enter "lifecycleofaladybug" into the search box.

3) Click the "Surf" button to see a list of websites.

With factsurfer, finding more information is just a click away.